WALTER TULL's Scrapbook

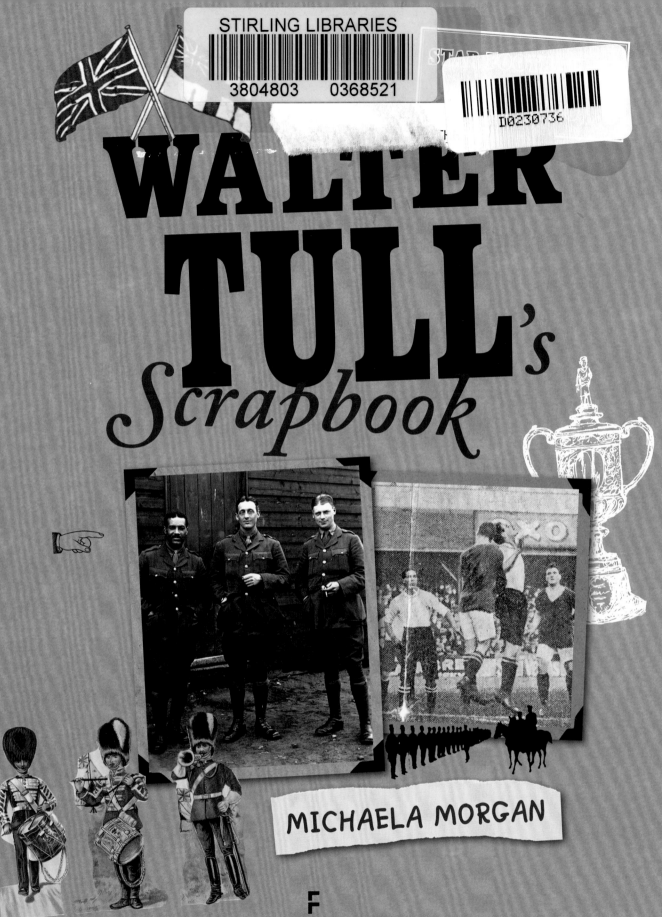

MICHAELA MORGAN

F

FRANCES LINCOLN
CHILDREN'S BOOKS

This is the true story of Walter Tull's life
presented as a fictionalised scrapbook and
using actual photos, documents and records.

To Tom Murphy for all his help and support - M.M.

Frances Lincoln Children's Books,
74-77 White Lion Street, London, N1 9PF
www.franceslincoln.com

First published in 2012 by Frances Lincoln Children's Books
This edition published in paperback in 2013

ISBN: 978-1-84780-491-4

Text © Michaela Morgan 2012
Drawings © Ian Benfold Hayward 2012

A CIP catalogue record for this book is available
from the British Library

3 5 7 9 8 6 4 2

Printed in China

Contents

My name is Walter Tull   4

The Home   6

Football!   8

Spurs   10

A New Start   12

Marching Off to War   14

A Christmas Miracle   16

The Battle Continues   18

My Birthday   20

Ordered to the Somme   22

An Officer!   24

Passchendaele   26

In Memory   30

Acknowledgements, websites, further reading   32

Picture acknowledgements   32

My name is Walter Tull. This is my scrapbook.

1888-1898

My oldest brother, William.

Edward, my brother – two years older than me.

My sis, Cecilia. (We call her Cissy sometimes.)

My dad

Baby Elsie. Possibly the noisiest baby in the world!

ME!
Walter Daniel John Tull.
Born 28th April 1888

My family

My big sister Bertha isn't in this photo. She died when she was a little girl. My mum isn't in the picture either.

Here she is. Her name was Alice and she was from a Folkestone family, the Palmers. I think she was the best mum in the world – but she kept getting ill and by the time the photo of us all was taken, she was dead. She died two weeks before my 7th birthday.

We all live together at

51 WALTON STREET,
HYTHE, FOLKESTONE,
ENGLAND,
THE WORLD.

My mum, Alice

I go to North Board School in Black Bull Road. The school is just at the top of our road. We can see the classrooms and playground from our front windows and I can walk there in a minute. My brother Eddie gets there in half a minute. He has longer legs.

England

Barbados

My dad, Daniel Tull, comes from **Barbados.**
It was a long journey across the sea to a new life in
Folkestone. On the way over, he worked as a ship's carpenter.

My dad's parents were slaves in Barbados. But my dad was never
a slave. He was a paid carpenter — and proud of it. He was a good
man and a hard worker, but he couldn't manage to work and keep
the house and children after my mum died, so my Aunty Clara came
to help run the house. She and my dad got married and she
became my stepmother. They had a baby girl, Miriam.
So there were lots of us. We all slept in two beds,
one for the boys and one for the girls.

10TH DECEMBER 1897.
DAD DIED.
HEART ATTACK.

Aunty Clara isn't my real mum, so we are now orphans.
Money is tight. Stepmum really tried, but she just couldn't
look after all of us. She has good friends in the local
Methodist church and they have found a place for us.
Me and my brother Eddie are being sent away on Valentine's
Day to be looked after at a Methodist Children's Home.

The Home
1898-1900

The children's home is miles away, in London. It's our first train journey ever – and the first time we've ever been out of Folkestone. The East End of London is very different from where we grew up. Everything is big and noisy. It's exciting, but frightening too. I tried to be brave when our step-mum waved goodbye and we went through the big iron gates into our new home.

The Home is enormous. It is a group of big houses each looked after by a "sister". Edward and I are both in the same house. It is carefully organised and everyone knows exactly what they have to do. We all have jobs.

Bonner Road Home

There are 320 children. We have our own school with lessons every day. Doctor Stephenson runs the Home. He is strict, but makes sure we have two hours off every evening. That's when I play cricket and, best of all, football. I am really good at football – I even made the Bonner Road School team!

BONNER ROAD

ME!

Bonner Road School team

6

My timetable

6.20 a.m. – Get up and make beds. Wash well and quickly (with VERY cold water).

Chores – Clean boots – at least 15 pairs, or wash floors. I prefer polishing boots. Scrubbing floors hurts your hands – and knees! When you finish your chores, Sister inspects your work and if you pass inspection, you go for breakfast.

Breakfast – Bread and marge with cocoa (with skin on top. Yuk!)

Prayers in the school chapel (or church in the town – twice on Sundays).

School – Lessons for the youngsters, plus training in printing or baking for the older children.

Lunch – One course – soup, pie or fish (plenty more skin. Yuk!)

School – Lessons for everyone. Arithmetic. Reading. Bible.

Personal hygiene – Thorough strip wash. Scrub. Then Sister's inspection of our scrubbed ears, necks, hands, nails.

5 p.m. tea – Bread and marge with cocoa (even more yuk!)

5 p.m. to 7 p.m. – Two hours' free time (cricket or football for me, plus writing letters home)

8 p.m. – Bed, lights out.

SUNLIGHT SOAP.

HOW TO WASH A FLOOR AT BONNER ROAD SCHOOL

Take a tin bucket, scrubbing brush,
cloth and bar of soap.
Fill bucket with cold water.
Scrub your line of floorboards.
Change the water after every fourth board.

I am learning to be a printer – so that I can earn my living when I leave the Home.
The best times here are when I get a letter from the family in Folkestone. We both get letters and cards and sometimes visits too.
That is the very best bit of all.

14th November 1900

Eddie has been adopted. He's leaving the Home and going all the way to Glasgow, in Scotland, to live with a dentist's family. It's hundreds of miles away. I am glad his new family are going to give him a good education and a chance in life, but still. . .

ME!

Now I'm on my own.

Good luck in your new home
Walter
I'll miss you

Football!
1900-1909

I'm finally out of Bonner Road. At first I was in a hostel run by the Methodists. Now I've moved into digs with a nice family. It's almost like a real home.

My cricket and football are being noticed. A friend suggested I write to **CLAPTON FOOTBALL CLUB** to ask for a trial. That was a hard letter to write. I wrote it over and over again until I got it right. Then it took some nerve to post it. But I have been given a trial and. . .

THEY WANT ME!

My record at Clapton F.C.

October 1908: first trial match. We win **6-1**.
December 26th 1908: I play for the first team.
1909: I am now a regular player and we win . . . EVERYTHING! We win the Football Association Amateur Challenge Cup, the London Senior Cup and the County Amateur Cup. An incredible record!!!

Six weeks ago I was playing in the Park for the Bonner Road School team. Now I am playing for **CLAPTON F.C.** – one of the best amateur teams in the country. I am training hard and making lots of progress.

F.G.O.Smart 1824

ME!

Clapton F.C. cup-winners

The newspapers are beginning to notice me and some of the big football clubs have noticed me too. . .

In April, **Tottenham Hotspur** asked me to try for their reserve team against West Ham and then **Brighton**. What a chance! I did well, so then I played for Spurs again in a friendly, and they have asked me to go on tour with them — to South America! For two whole months!!!

In 1909 I set off on an enormous ship for a football tour of South America — Argentina and Uruguay.

R. M. S. "Araguaya"

Imagine me — a big star on a big ship going to Argentina!

Tottenham Hotspur F.C. have just asked me to sign for them. I wasn't sure about becoming a professional and taking money for playing sport. I think sport should build your character and make you stronger in body and mind. But in the end I did sign. It is better to be paid out in the open rather than pretending to be an amateur and taking money under the table, which some clubs have offered me. It is always best to be honest.

My football kit

Shirt — thick, warm and good for a cold day — but when it's wet it's like wearing a heavy, damp sponge

Shorts — we call them "knickers". They are long and loose and they soak up the mud

Boots — heavy leather with great big studs. They can really hurt if you get kicked

Ball — made of thick leather with a big strong lace. It soaks up water and weight. When it's wet, it's like heading a brick. Ouch!

2

Spurs
1909-1911

On 20th July 1909 I signed for **Tottenham Hotspur.** They say I'm the first black British professional out field player.

I got a signing-on fee. TEN POUNDS! Ten whole pounds — and a wage of FOUR POUNDS a week. This is the maximum — and they gave it to me! While waiting for the football season to start I played cricket. It's a good way to spend a sunny day. The Spurs players took on the **CHELSEA** team, and I scored a good number of runs — and took a couple of wickets. We footballers like to play cricket in the off season.

Me in my Spurs kit. A proud day.

Tottenham Hotspur Football Club, 1911-12.

ME IN THE SPURS TEAM

ME AGAINST MANCHESTER UNITED

For my first Spurs match I took over from Vivian Woodward, the Spurs star centre forward and Olympic champ, so I had to do well. It was Spurs' first ever Division One game after promotion. I played against **MANCHESTER UNITED.**

Final score: a **2-2** draw.

ME

Hotspur.

1911.

p.m.

3
Burns.

6
Marshall

abe
Walker

15
Clark

16
Tull

19
Morris

ANT.
and P. REEVES.

BRISTOL

I had a terrible time at the BRISTOL match.
Every time I got the ball, the crowd broke into
jeers and insults about my skin colour. It was
hard to carry on, but I made it to the end
of the game.

A journalist wrote about the match in the
LONDON FOOTBALL STAR.

The ✦ Star

LONDON, MONDAY, NOVEMBER 11, 1912.   ONE

Football and Colour Prejudice

. . .Tull is the Hotspurs' most brainy forward. Candidly, he
has much to contend with on account of his colour. His tactics
were absolutely beyond reproach, but he became the butt of
the ignorant partisan . . . a section of the spectators made a
cowardly attack upon him in language
lower than Billingsgate . . . Let me tell
the Bristol hooligans . . . that Tull is
so clean in mind and method as to be
a model for all white men who play
football. Tull was the best forward
on the field.

ME

17

TOBACCO, CIGARS AND CIGARETTES

And the Finest Value for Money
IN THE DISTRICT

Can be obtained from the Old-Established
Firm of TOBACCONISTS

WILLIAM ROE & CO.,
(Outside Bruce Grove Station).

515-7, HIGH ROAD,
TOTTENHAM.

16

W. D. TULL—Umpire or Inside Forward.
height 5ft. 8ins, weight 11st. Played for an
Team and Clapton F.C., helped Clapt
Amateur Cup and the London County An
He gained 3 gold medals in his first yea
football.

C. H. TURRALL.—Outside Right. The
County Captain. Age 23, height 5ft. 11ins.,
11st. 5lbs. Played for Braintree, Chelmsford
Chelmsford Town and Essex County.

ON YOU SPURS

I know I played well — everybody says so, and I tried
not to react to all the insults that people threw at me.
I kept my head . . . but somehow I'm losing heart. I try
not to let it get to me, but it's hard.

11

A New Start
1911-1914

I've been through a bad patch where I lost sight of my aims and my energy leaked away. I lost heart, I lost form. But bit by bit I've regained my spirits, gathered my courage and started again. I've been transferred (for a huge fee) to NORTHAMPTON – a big team these days.

LIVE LIKE A LION
Proud and Strong.

I've settled down well at Northampton, made some good friends and played some great games. I am popular with the team and the crowd. I've now played more that 100 times for Northampton. And I've scored four goals in one match! Best of all, GLASGOW RANGERS want me to play for them. They're one of the top teams in Scotland. If I transfer to Glasgow I'll be living near my brother Edward! I can hardly wait.

THE G

Extract from

and GIVE
PLAY t
and JOIN

"Drinking is pre-
judicial to
victory."
—Lord Roberts.

"Abstin
nece
the
effi
—Ad

"We have to fight three enemies—the Germans, the Austrian
but the greatest of these is Drink."—Chancellor of the Exchequer

PATRIOTIC PLEDGE:

In order that I may be of the great
to my Country at this time of nat
Promise by God's help to absta
nd of the war.

WAR

There's been talk in the papers about trouble in Europe. Now it looks as if we are at war with Germany and the Army is looking for volunteers. Posters have started to advertise for a special battalion made up of footballers. When I saw the posters I didn't think twice. I have to stand up for my country.

No more football for me for a while. No transfer to Glasgow.

We are at war.

Marching Off to War
December 1914

I've joined up. I am now **Private Walter Tull** of the 17th Middlesex Regiment — the Footballers Battalion — ready to fight for King and Country. Everyone in the Football Battalion is either a player, a supporter or has worked for a club. We are training and parading and marching. I have a very different sort of kit now — in khaki. All the soldiers in my unit are good men and I'm sure we will do well.

My uniform

Peaked cap

Heavy khaki jacket with room for a shirt and a sweater — or several — underneath

Plenty of pockets and webbing cloth belts

We also carry a huge, heavy coat called a "great coat"

Putties — to stop your trouser-legs getting caught on wire

Boots - Very strong, very heavy, very uncomfortable

Canvas bag with gasmask

Plus kit bag
containing ground sheet and blanket, rifle with canvas cover to keep out mud, mess tin (that's what we eat our food in) and tool for digging

All this stuff is so heavy that when we tried the full kit on Skinny Albert, he just fell over backwards and lay there waving his legs in the air like a helpless beetle!

At last we are off to France. After months of training and marching and polishing we are going to the front. We should be in the trenches by Christmas.

We keep our courage high by singing as we march.

There is lots to learn. It's a whole new world in the front line — with its own new words.

My battalion marching

Pack Up Your Troubles In Your Old Kit Bag

Smile!

Battle phrase book

Whizz-bang — Enemy cannon. It's named after the sound it makes. If you hear a WHIZZ, it will be followed by a BANG, and you'll have copped it.

Copped it — Been killed.

Jack Johnson — A shot from a heavy cannon, (named after a heavyweight boxer, because it packs a very big punch!)

No Man's Land — The area between your trenches and the enemy's. A very, very dangerous place.

Over the top — Leaving your trenches to attack the enemy. Maybe the last time you see your friends alive.

Shrapnel — The jagged bits of cannon shell that come flying at you. Very sharp and very nasty.

Sniper — A soldier who shoots at anything sticking out of a trench. It is a very good idea to keep your head down!

Stand to — Standing in your trenches, waiting for an enemy attack. There's a stand-to twice every day, at first light and at dusk.

When the whistle blows — Not like a referee's whistle! This is the officer's signal to leave the trenches and attack.

It's got your name on it — The bullet or cannon shell that's coming to get you.

Trench Foot — Horrible foot-rot that you get from standing in mud and water for weeks and never drying out.

A Christmas Miracle
December 1915

I'm in the Front Line. I'm cold. I'm wet. I'm muddy. I'm exhausted. My ears are still ringing with the sounds of explosions. I've heard and seen things I could never have imagined — not even in my worst nightmares. But I've heard of a miracle, too. . . Private Jones told us about it. We were huddled in our trench trying to shelter from the biting cold when he started his story:

"It was cold and frosty and almost midnight on December 24th last year. Christmas Eve — and I was spending it in an icy trench. I saw something glimmering not far away. Then I saw another glimmer and another. The enemy soldiers had lit candles all around their trench! That's when we heard it — a clear German voice ringing out in the frosty night, singing a Christmas carol. We all held our breath and listened as the German soldier sang his version of 'Silent Night'. The last line rang out clear as a bell.

The Christmas Truce

It was heartbreakingly beautiful in that murky setting. Back home in Wales they call me 'Jones the Voice', so I was the one who stood up and sang 'Silent Night' back to them. Then it began. We all sang together, British and Germans celebrating peace on Earth and goodwill to all men. We shouted Christmas greetings.

" *Merry Christmas* "

" *Frohe Weinhachten* "

Finally, one by one, we crawled out of our muddy holes and walked across No Man's Land to shake hands and exchange greetings with the enemy. One of the men had a football, so we played a match with the Germans! There weren't many rules and there were about 50 men on each side — but such spirit! No shots were fired that night. Nor the next day."

FOOTBALL BOOTS

A CHRISTMAS DAY BEHIND THE FIRING LINE

PUZZLE
Find the Colonel

I found Private Jones' story hard to believe, but later I heard that peace had broken out like this all along the battlefront. Up to 100,000 men had stopped shooting and started talking and giving presents. The Germans and the British gave each other pound notes or mark notes, cigarettes, sweets and even coat buttons.

Compliments of the Season

It was a Christmas miracle.

The Battle Continues
1916

News today: Ben copped it. The first footballer in our battalion to die. He was a strong player and a good man.

R.I.P. Ben Butler.
Queen's Park Rangers centre half, Soldier in Footballer's Battalion 17th Middlesex Regiment. Killed in action.

ON ACTIVE SERVICE.

Y.M.C.A.

Hush, here comes a Whizz-bang
And it's making right for you.
Now, you soldier men, get down those stairs,
Down in your dug-outs and say your prayers,
Hush, here comes a Whizz-bang
And it's making right for you.
And you'll see all the wonders of No Man's Land
If a Whizz-bang hits you.

Some kids lie about their age in order to join up.
They are often the first to cop it.

Notes from the trenches

Morning – Get up very early after a night of snatched sleep – often woken by the cold, by the scuttling rats or the sound of shells or shots.

Try to straighten up and get moving.

Stand to, with bayonets drawn, watching the opposite trenches.

Fire a few rounds at the enemy (usually you can't see them). Some of the men call this the Morning Hate.

Stand down, get some breakfast and keep warm.

Try to find time to write home and clean my rifle. Keep my head down and take care not to get shot by a sniper.

Look for a spot of sunshine and stand in it for a short moment of hope and prayer.

Repair a trench wall. Clean the mud off my face – often no water to wash in.

Hungry for my dinner – tinned bully beef, hard biscuits and tea. It's not much but I'm desperate for it.

Always a tinge of fear. If a shell has your name on it you are done for. You never know when it is coming. Tired. The men try to joke with each other and pass time chasing the rats away. We try to keep our chins up.

I pray to God I can do my duty and then go home to peace.

Evening stand to. Hope for a bit of warmth and sleep without too many fleas or explosions to disturb us.

Dream of dry socks.

b.

c.

f.

Trench

Scale 1:10,000

Waiting in the trenches

I have been promoted three times. I am 26 years old and I am now a Lance Sergeant. That means I do a Sergeant's job but don't get his pay. I hope that next time I get a proper promotion.

28th April 1916 – My Birthday

My presents:
- ✓ Nine days on the front without rest.
- ✓ A big box of exhaustion.
- ✓ Seven months in France without leave.
- ✓ Terrible nightmares.

The other day I woke up feeling terribly ill.
My ears were ringing and my body was shaking.
I could hardly stand up. My head was foggy and
full of the sights I had seen . . . explosions,
men blown to bits, drowning in mud. . .
I tried to start the day but I couldn't.

A Joyful Birthday.

On this thy Birthday which has come
May happiness be thine
May azu...

A birthday card I received

Transporting the wounded

My officer knew I was not the
sort to make a fuss so he sent me
off to the nearest hospital. When
I got there they gave me a bed of
wire netting – and I could lie on it
FULL LENGTH, stretched out.
This is LUXURY after crouching in
the trenches night after night.

The nurses gave
me evaporated
milk to make me
stronger. The
doctor decided to send me back to Britain. He said
I had "shell shock". I'm not sure what this means.
Maybe the endless explosions have shocked my system.
What bliss it is to sleep. . .

Armour's
TRADE Veribest
EVAPORATED
MILK

Hospital train

The Rose of No Man's Land

Words by Jack Caddigan
Music by James A. Brennan

Published by LEO FEIST, INC. Feist Building, New York

ENLIST TO-DAY

In hospital back in Britain

I'm surrounded by men with what's called "Trench Fever" or "Shell Shock". The doctors have lots of official names for it, like Acute Mania, Neurasthenia, Acute Exhaustion. They all mean the same thing — men with shattered nerves who shake as if they have a permanent fever, men who dream and scream. They have become empty shells, shivering and shaking at the slightest noise. One of the doctors told me that many soldiers don't recover. Not ever. But I did.

September 1916

It has taken three months, but now I'm heading back to the battle front.

Original

CONFIDENTIAL.

PROCEEDINGS OF A MEDICAL BOARD

Army Form A. 45.

(Rank and Name)...... Walter Tull

by order of...... A.C.I. 428 .... (Corps)......

Ordered to the Somme
October 1916

This place is a vision of Hell. The smells. . . the sounds. . .

The battle of the Somme (a river in northern France) has been going on for months. The place is a quagmire of mud. We live in our hole in the ground as if we have already been buried. We are attacking hard, and the enemy are defending every step of the way. I run through mud and barbed wire, explosions, machine gun fire. Men die around me, friends. . .

I see terrible, terrible things. . . My own regiment started out with 400 men. Only 79 were still alive when we left. And I was one of the lucky few.

ROB, Monday, July 3, 1916.

ADVANCE STILL CONTINUES : 7,000 PRISONERS

...ne Daily Mirror

...ED CIRCULATION LARGER THAN THAT OF ANY OTHER DAILY PICTURE PAPER

One Halfpenny.

Registered at the G.P.O.
as a Newspaper.

MONDAY, JULY 3, 1916.

...OFFICIAL PHOTOGRAPH OF THE PREPARATIONS FOR THE
...REAT BRITISH ADVANCE ON THE WESTERN FRONT.

One of our new heavy guns and crew who have assisted in preparing the way for the attack.—(Official photograph, Crown copyright reserved.)

Duke Albrecht of Württemberg.

DAILY SKETCH.

GUARANTEED DAILY NETT SALE MORE THAN 1,000,0

No. 2,291. LONDON, WEDNESDAY, JULY 12, 1916.

HOW OUR LADS WENT T

Men of the Worcester Regiment photographed on their way to the front line to take their place

A Roll Call in the trenches on the afternoon of July 1.—(Official Photographs.)

You have read the story of how British Troops went into battle with a smile and a cheer. The top photograph shows that the wonderful stories of our war correspondents, our official and semi-official eye-witnesses were not exaggerated. The camera shows you plainly the spirit of our men.

Rescuing horses in the mud

Roses of Picardy
SONG

WORDS BY
FRED. E. WEATHERLY

MUSIC BY
HAYDN WOOD

PRICE 60 CENTS
2/6 NET CASH

CHAPPELL & CO LTD.
MELBOURNE   LONDON   SYDNEY

FOR THE COUNTRIES OF NORTH AMERICA
CHAPPELL-HARMS, INC.
NEW YORK

LOW
MEDIUM
HIGH

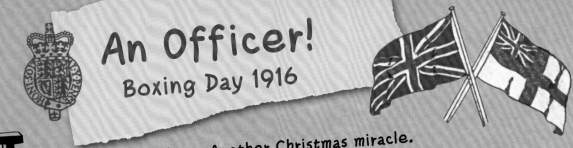

An Officer!
Boxing Day 1916

The most amazing thing. Another Christmas miracle. I am being sent on leave (my first official leave since joining the Army) and I am to be trained as an officer.

Me – a real officer and a gentleman!

My commanders have been very impressed by me. They say I keep a cool head and a strong heart. I have one big worry. I've heard that black men cannot be officers in the British Army. I've looked it up – this is what I found:

14. These officers are subject to recall to Army Service in a time of national emergency, and become subject to military law in the circumstances mentioned in s. 175 (10) of the Army Act.

15. The Special Reserve of Officers is a branch of the Reserve of Officers established by Royal Warrant (a). This Reserve of Officers is designed to ensure that all units, services and departments of the regular forces shall be complete in officers on mobilization; to make good the wastage which will occur in the regular forces in war, and to provide officers for special reserve units. Militia officers received commissions in this reserve when the militia was transferred to the Special Reserve in 1908 (b).

Commissions in the Special Reserve of Officers are given to qualified candidates who are natural born or naturalised British subjects of pure European descent.

16. In the Cavalry, Royal Field and Garrison Artillery, Royal Engineers, Postal Section, Motor Cyclist Section, Foot Guards, Army Service Corps, Royal Army Medical Corps and Army Veterinary Corps such officers are borne supplementary to those corps; in the North or South Irish Horse, King Edward's Horse (The King's Oversea Dominions Regiment), the Antrim or Cork R.G.A., the Royal Anglesey or Royal Monmouthshire Royal Engineers they are borne on the strength of those units, and in the infantry they are either borne on the strength of the Special Reserve battalion, or supplementary to a regiment.

17. Except in the case of candidates who have previously served in the regular army all appointments are made on probation in the rank of subaltern. During the period of probation an officer is usually attached to a regular unit, and if he is reported upon favourably and passes the required examination he is confirmed

A Commission in the Special Reserve of Officers published by His Majesty's Stationery Office, 1912.

Visiting my brother

In my case, it seems they have thrown away the rule book. This could make me the first black officer in the British Army. Something for the record books! I'm off to officer training school in Scotland to train for my commission – and I will have a chance to see Edward. At last.

Despite military regulations forbidding "any negro or person of colour" being commissioned as an officer, I am now **2nd Lieutenant Walter Tull** – and here I am in my new uniform.

An officer at war

Imagine – me an officer with my old battalion! It is a very responsible job. I now have my men to look after and I work hard to keep their spirits up. They seem to like me and I have a very good sergeant to help me.

Me as an Officer

<u>My Uniform</u>

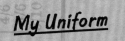

Officer's tie

Officer's shirt

Officer's leather belt and cross belt

2nd Lieutenant's badge on cuffs

I even have my own servant to look after me (he's called a "batman"), and I have a bit more to eat, but it is still very, very hard work. There are some tough battles ahead. I pray I do well.

Passchendaele Belgium
1917-1918

June 1917.
We've had a hard time capturing some high ground called the Messines Ridge. Our lads planted a huge bomb under enemy lines. We won the high ground and captured 80 prisoners, but half the battalion's men were killed or wounded.

July 1917.
Again we are trying to capture some high ground, this time around Pilkem – also known as Passchendaele. Me and my troop of lads did everything we were asked to and I suppose we won, but we lost a lot of men. So many killed! I can say this here, but I wouldn't tell anyone at home. The numbers killed are too terrible.

September 1917
Now we are attacking another hill held by the enemy. It's called the Menin Ridge. My men do wonderfully well and we capture the trenches as ordered. I am very proud of my soldiers, but even when we are winning, we lose men. Today – 15 killed, 121 wounded and 23 missing just from my battalion.

I've been volunteering for dangerous missions into enemy trenches with a few hand-picked men. I don't write home about this. Edward would be worried if he knew.

I've heard a rumour from an officer who knows someone who works for the War Office in London. They say thousands and thousands of soldiers have been killed — many more than they say in the newspapers. They say we lost nearly 60,000 men by lunchtime when we attacked on the Somme. All those men dead in the mud. And after that, 420,000 British troops were killed in fighting over four months at the same place. Battles that the newspapers claim have been victories don't seem like victories to us.

What the War Office person says matches what we have all seen at the front — we lose men every day, and win a few feet of mud.

Giavera, Italy,   October

I've been sent to Italy. When I think that I started out as an orphan in London and now I've travelled to Argentina, France and Italy. We are in northern Italy, near a place called Giavera. We are on a hill overlooking the River Piave. Italy is not how I imagined it. It is quieter than the war in France, but a muddy trench is a muddy trench no matter which country you're in. And still the shots ring out and the shells fall. It's cold here and very, very wet.

Planning the next move

← GIAVERA

January 1918

I am leading many raids across the river. It's dangerous. Yesterday a senior officer came and saw the good work my men and I did on a raid into enemy lines. He has mentioned me in official dispatches. It makes me feel really good, and proud of my men.

This is what the officer said: "I wish to place on record my appreciation of your gallantry and coolness. You were one of the first to cross the river prior to the raid on 1st to 2nd January 1918, and during the raid you took the covering party of the main body across and brought them back without a casualty in spite of heavy fire."

I've been told that I've been recommended for a medal — the Military Cross. I wonder if I'll get it?

One of our brave horses

Beugry, France
March 1918

The battalion only had a short stay in Italy, and here we are back in the French mud. I can hardly imagine life without mud. I've seen a horse drown in mud. Men have drowned in it too.

We are back near the Somme, almost where we started. It looks as if there will be a major attack by the enemy. I pray to God that we can stop them.

24th March 1918

Terrible news. The enemy have launched an appalling attack and we've had to retreat. It is very confusing. We are being shelled all the time. Many of our men are dead, even the battalion commander. We keep retreating.

I must do my duty. I must play the game. . .

28

[handwritten letter fragment, top left]

...5th last.
...ing at present in command
(the Captain was wounded...
...to say how popular he...
...the Battalion. He w...
...conscientious; he had...
...ed for the "Military C...
...certainly earned it; th...
...my...
&...

POST OFFICE TELEGRAPHS.

This Form must accompany any inquiry respecting this Telegram.

Delivery and Charges
Means
Distance
Collected
Paid out
C. OR B.
Prefix

Sent, or Sent out ..... No. of Telegram 2202
At ..... M.
To .....
By .....
GLASGOW 17 AP
Received here at 8.38...

7.40 OHMS BUCKINGHAM PALACE 48 =

TULL 419 ST VINCENT ST GLW =

THE KING AND QUEEN DEEPLY REGRET THE LOSS YOU AND THE
ARMY HAVE SUSTAINED BY THE DEATH OF 2 ND LT W D
TULL IN THE SERVICE OF HIS COUNTRY THEIR MAJESTIES TRULY
SYMPATHISE WITH YOU IN YOUR SORROW = KEEPER OF THE
PRIVY PURSE :

Charges to pay s. d.

Received at ..... From ..... By .....
663 ..... CT 419 22 :

No. of Telegram 1 P.O./11

I certify that this Telegram is sent on the service of the

W O

(Signature) .....

hereof. ..... Street

Dated Stamp.

[second telegram, handwritten]

...ddlesex Regt ..... Lieut W.D. Tull
March Twentyfifth killed in action the Army
Council express Sympathy

FROM { SECRETARY WAR OFFICE

The Name and Address of the Sender, IF NOT TO BE TELEGRAPHED, should be written in the space provided at the Back of the Form.

2nd Lieutenant Walter Daniel John Tull was killed
on 25th March 1918 during the Second Battle of the
Somme. He was 29 years old.
He was shot while crossing No Man's Land. His men
tried to recover his body. Three times they ran
into No Man's Land, but were forced back by enemy
fire. His body was never recovered.

In memory

Walter Tull

Born: Folkestone, 1888

Orphaned: Aged nine

Footballer: The first Black British out field Player. Star of Clapton, Tottenham Hotspurs, Northampton Town. Signed for Glasgow Rangers but never played.

Soldier/Lance Sergeant: 1915-16

The first black officer in the British Army 1917. Recommended for the Military Cross, Italy 1918. This was never awarded.

Died: in Northern France during the German Spring Offensive of 1918, aged 29.

Memorial: Walter Tull's name is inscribed on the Arras Memorial to the Missing in France, along with 35,000 other fallen soldiers.

W.D.J. Tull

Though ridiculed the his actions barriers of ignorance of colour
equality with deny people their contemporaries.
His life stands testa- ment to a
determination to confront those
people and those obst- acles that
sought to diminish him and the
World in which he lived.
It reveals a man thou- gh rendered
breathless in his prime, whose
strong heart still beats loudly.
This memorial marks an area of
reflective space as a Garden of
Remembra- nce.

ACKNOWLEDGEMENTS

Grateful thanks to Tom Murphy for all his assistance, and to Mr Duncan Finlayson and the family of Walter Tull. Particular acknowledgement is due to Phil Vasili for his detailed and original research and his book *Walter Tull, 1888-1918, Officer, Footballer* (Raw Press, 2010); *The Imperial War Museum Book of The Western Front*, Malcolm Brown (Pan, 2001); *When The Whistle Blows: the Story of the Footballers' Battalion in the Great War*, Andrew Riddoch and John Kemp (J.H. Haynes & Co. Ltd, 2011).

WEBSITES

General (American) facts http://lou_wwl.tripod.com/mywwltrench/id3.html
General statistics http://en.wikipedia.org/wiki/World_War_I_casualties

FURTHER READING

Respect! Michaela Morgan (Barrington Stoke, 2005)
Walter Tull: Footballer, Soldier, Hero, Dan Lyndon (Collins Big Cat, 2011)

PICTURE ACKNOWLEDGEMENTS

Action for Children 6 top and bottom; Bruce Castle Museum (Haringey Culture, Libraries and Learning)10 top/back cover and centre; Maria Charalambous 31; Duncan Finlayson Family Archive front cover centre, 4 top and bottom, 10 bottom/front cover, 11 top/title page, 24 centre right/back cover and bottom, 25 top/title page and bottom, 29 letter top left, telegram centre, 30; Imperial War Museums 12-13 top poster (Art. IWM PST 12126), 16 centre (detail, Q 50719), 18 top left (CO 924), centre right (detail, Q 5935) and bottom right (detail, Q 1284), 19 right (detail, Q 32896), 20 left (detail, Q 8752), 22 right (detail, CO 198), 23 top right (detail, Q 3249) and bottom (detail, Q 4501), 26 top left (detail, Q 2756) and bottom/front cover centre right (details, Q3014), 27 left, painting by Sydney W. Carline (Art. IWM ART 2677), and right (detail, Q 26509), 28 left (detail, Q 5717); John Frost Newspapers 13 bottom left, 22 left, 23 top left; Courtesy of Jeremy Kemp 21 top; Paul Reed 14-15 top; Tottenham Hotspur Football Club 10-11 team programme, 11 team programme.